Guinea Pigs
and
Chinchillas

Ken Denham

John Bartholomew and Son Limited
Edinburgh

© John Bartholomew & Son Ltd, 1977
First published in Great Britain 1977 by
John Bartholomew and Son Ltd., 12 Duncan Street,
Edinburgh, EH9 1TA

Reprinted 1982

ISBN 0 7028 1075 4

Printed in Great Britain by John Bartholomew & Son Limited

Contents

PART ONE: CAVIES (GUINEA PIGS)

PART TWO: CHINCHILLAS

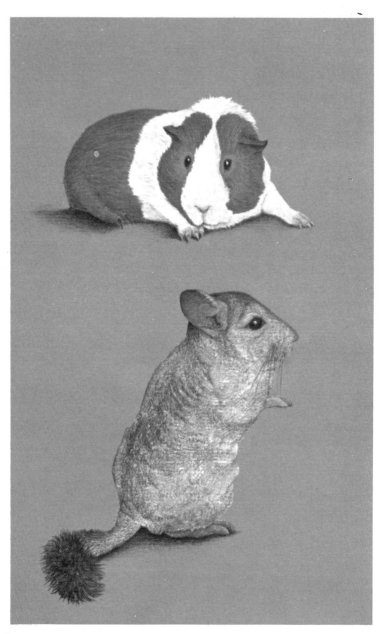

Part One

Cavies (Guinea Pigs)

Introduction

Anyone attending a pet trade fair or looking down the columns of either specialist magazines or newspapers that advertise pets, can see that pet keeping is an extremely active interest both with young people and adults. Acquiring a pet in a household, however, does not always come about for the right reasons. Often a pet will be a gift from someone who no longer wants it or perhaps saw it in a pet dealer's shop and thought that the new owner might enjoy it. Undoubtedly the appeal of pets on display in shops helps a great deal to sell the pet. Shopkeepers rely on the impulse buying power that his stock influences. Street markets where pets are sold seldom advertise their stock and rely almost entirely on passing trade.

Buying any kind of pet in this way, however, is fraught with problems. Gifts of pets are seldom appreciated unless previously agreed to, half the fun and interest in buying a pet is choosing one which appeals particularly to you and that is just the pleasure you have been deprived of by someone else. People who give pets may not have taken into consideration the pet's requirements and if such a pet will fit into the new owner's household.

All prospective pet keepers must consider a few basic points before taking on the responsibility of another life.

First and foremost, 'why do you want a pet?' The reasons can be many and quite varied; however, it should never be simply a matter of having a fashionable pet like your neighbour's or someone else's you envy. This type of pet keeping is often doomed from the start, once the fashion has worn itself out.

For older people pets can provide a new interest, a field of study in their spare time or even take the place of friends or family who have moved away and are no longer around to provide companionship.

For young people pet keeping can provide a real source of learning; studying all the materials and data available on the history and zoology of pet animals is only the beginning of what can be added to the knowledge gained from personal experience. Choice of pets is always up to the individual but such considerations as the cost of the animal, feeding, cleaning and general maintenance of its housing, breeding possibilities and the time and money available to do all these things, particularly if you also enjoy holidays or occasional weekends away from home, must be given careful thought.

Taking all these things into consideration. Cavies or Guinea Pigs as they are popularly known, are really an excellent choice of pet for most people. They are strong, sturdy little creatures and even when only a few days old are active and appear exact miniatures of the adults, unlike many other mammals. Their feeding and housing requirements are simple to maintain, they can be handled easily even by young children, they are clean with no odour, reproduce without fuss and the youngsters, if not required, will be readily taken up by other pet keepers.

Chapter 1

History and Origins

The domestic Guinea Pig, whose scientific name is *Cavia porcellus*, seems to have originated in South America, where in fact some species still exist today. Apparently the Andean Indian kept and bred them for food hundreds of years ago and they were taken from there to Europe about 400 years ago by Spanish sailors, probably as a source of fresh meat on board ship and then eventually kept as pets.

Cavies are true Rodents which is a scientifically classified order of mammals which contains over 1,700 different species. It has been said that two out of every five species of mammals belongs to the order of Rodents.

The word 'Rodent' is derived from the Latin word RODERE which means 'to gnaw'. The order includes such animals as rats and mice, squirrels, marmots, chipmunks etc., but the Cavy or Guinea Pig is more closely related to the Porcupines and Agoutis. They are also quite closely related to the largest living Rodent the Capybara of South America, which appears to be a large Guinea Pig about the size of a young domestic pig and weighing more than 100 lb but unlike the Guinea Pigs it has slightly webbed feet and spends a great deal of time in water, though it is equally inoffensive.

Rodents have a very specialised dentition enabling them to gnaw through materials such as wood at a fairly rapid rate. The four front teeth, called incisors, are both chisel-like in their shape and the action in which they are involved. The front of these teeth, often brown in colour, is made up of a hard, strong enamel whereas behind this the rest of the tooth is of a softer material known as dentine. When used normally, the teeth wear unevenly, the back of the tooth wears away more quickly, forming a chisel shape towards the front of the tooth. There

Capybara
This South American animal is the largest living rodent relative of the cavy and grows to the size of a labrador dog. These animals are kept in a number of zoos and are well worth further study.

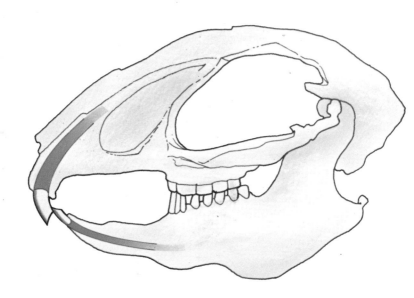

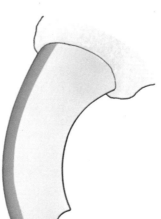

The rodent's incisors used for cutting and gnawing are constantly in use and wear quickly. They grow continuously throughout the animal's lifetime. The soft dentine wears away quicker than the hard enamel at the front of the incisors, causing the constant sharpening of the teeth by grinding them into a chisel shape.

are no canine teeth or premolars in the jaws of Rodents as there are in Carnivores. The gap is called a diestema and this is used to effect by Rodents as it enables the animal to draw in its cheeks and close off the rest of the mouth while gnawing at tree bark etc., also protecting its other teeth by allowing them to rest with the aid of a complicated muscle mechanism which allows its jaws to move at the front without its grinding teeth or molars being affected.

Guinea Pigs are quite hardy animals and some people keep them outside all year round. However, some of the more inbred varieties would not tolerate such conditions and would be subject to chills and then catch cold or worse. Also, the heavier furred varieties would become unsightly if allowed to roam around.

Normally Guinea Pigs do not suffer very much from diseases or illnesses; however, breeding from very young stock or consistent inbreeding does weaken the strain and they may then become susceptible to illness. The compact body of this roly-poly animal assists in its heat retention although Guinea Pigs can suffer from heat exhaustion if allowed too much sunshine or other forms of direct heat. Therefore, we have in the Guinea Pig an interesting animal, easily handled even by small children, with no difficult diet, housing or illness problems, possibly the ideal pet.

Chapter 2

Housing

In all forms of pet keeping a great deal of consideration must be given to housing the animals. The person responsible for the maintenance of the pet must ensure that the animal's home has all the comforts that it needs and is practical from a feeding, sleeping and exercise point of view and can provide suitable accommodation for breeding and rearing young at a later date if required. Also, cleaning at regular intervals is so much easier if due consideration has been given to the design and layout of the housing.

Most pet Guinea Pigs live out their lives in hutches and these are a familiar sight in most pet shops. The usual hutch consists of a long box with about two-thirds of the front covered with wire mesh and the rest of the front consisting of a door. Sometimes the roof of the hutch is covered with a roofing felt or protective waterproofing material.

Apart from the specialist animal hutch builders whose products rarely appear in pet dealers' shops, few of the hutches offered are really very practical as they are often made from unsuitable materials such as plywood or unseasoned timber. They are generally too small for family use and are usually expensive. Specialist builders are usually even more expensive but they make very practical, strong cages and hutches that will last for many years. People who make this type of product advertise in specialist journals that appeal only to the fur and feather trade and hobbyist. The local newsagent is likely to be able to get current copies for you. Otherwise an established Guinea Pig breeder would know where to buy hutches suitable for your needs. However, undoubtedly the best method of getting your pets housed is to build your own hutches from good, strong wood about $\frac{1}{2}''$ thick ($1\frac{1}{2}$ cm). These can be designed to fit particular requirements, for instance, if the animals are to be kept in a shed, garden hut or garage then there is no need to put a rainproof roof on top of the hutch. At this point it should be mentioned that garages *can* be unsuitable and even dangerous places in which to house pets as fumes from car exhausts, petrol, paint and many other chemicals can prove fatal to all kinds of animals and even plants.

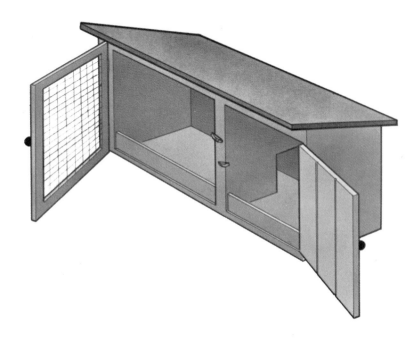

Hutches are designed according to the needs of both the pet keeper and the cavies. Breeding and rearing hutches need to be larger than those designed to keep single show specimens.
Keeping the hutches free from vermin such as mice is difficult, but not impossible, covering all climbing surfaces with sheet metal helps a great deal. Double wiring is effective yet costly.
Preventing the entry of animals that may burrow into a grass run type of housing, can best be done by attaching wire netting to the whole of the base. Grass soon grows through and hides the netting. Important reminder: hutches must have warm, dry quarters for the animal to retire to when necessary.

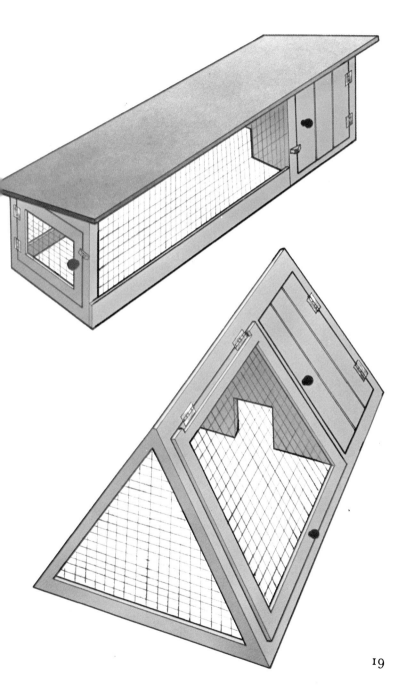

The design of your first hutch is most important, assuming you are going to keep your Guinea Pigs in the garden or yard outside; it must protect your pet from being annoyed by other animals if necessary, as some dogs and cats will cause havoc with smaller animals, though most will become used to them and accept them as part of the family after quite a short time. Raising the hutch off the ground helps to prevent this kind of nuisance and also assists the owner to clean, feed and study the animals. Therefore, an old table or cut down chair or stool could act as a stand for the hutch, or else you could make one to suit your own requirements. It is probably inadvisable to put legs on your first hutch for at least one good reason: you may wish to build more hutches at a later stage to the same pattern as your first and then if this is taken into consideration, stacking your hutches on top of each other is possible, saving space and making all the servicing much easier.

Sizes of hutches vary and you may have to modify your plans according to the site where you expect to keep your pets. Taking these things into consideration most experienced Guinea Pig keepers would aim to allow approximately $1\frac{1}{2}$ sq. ft. of floor space for each animal (approximately 45 sq. cm). Therefore, a hutch with a floor measuring $3' \times 1\frac{1}{2}'$ (approximately 90×45 cm) would be very suitable for three animals or a young family with their mother. The height of the cage inside should be about 15″ (40 cm approximately) though the cage may well have a sloping roof to allow rain water to run off towards the back.

The hutch should preferably be designed with two compartments with a suitable entrance cut out of the divider to allow the animals to gain access to both parts of the cage, placing the cut out entrance towards the back of the cage assists in weatherproofing the sleeping quarters which should take up approximately one-third of the total area of the hutch. A two door arrangement on the front of the hutch is very practical. One of the doors should be solid, completely enclosing the sleeping quarters, whereas the other door should consist of a frame of wood covered with wire mesh with holes of less than one inch (approximately $2\frac{1}{2}$ cm) across. If you are likely to get mice or rats or other small rodents causing a nuisance by stealing and fouling up the food provided for your pets, then special precautions are necessary. Wire mesh of much smaller gauge, helps to a certain extent but may not always prevent young mice or small species from gaining access. Nailing a strip of smooth sheet metal across all points where the pest might climb and enter is a considerable help and double netting is another method to be considered.

To prevent bedding, foodstuffs and even the animals falling out of the hutch when the doors are opened, a board about $4''$ high (10 cm approximately) can be made to slot into channels on the inside of the hutch. Other fittings should include a water bottle with a metal drinking tube attached to the front of the wire and an unspillable food bowl of metal or pottery. Guinea Pigs have strong teeth so all kinds of plastic materials can be destroyed by these animals in a very short time and may prove toxic if eaten. Even soft metal drinking tubes suffer after months of wear and stainless steel is highly recommended though expensive. The floor of the hutch is usually covered with a layer of sawdust, but this should not be too deep as it can get into the eyes of the Guinea Pigs and cause damage. Perhaps a little more than $\frac{1}{4}''$ in depth is sufficient (1 cm approximately). Bedding can consist of meadow hay and some of this may be eaten if not enough is supplied as a supplement to the animal's normal diet.

There are many alternatives to this type of housing and breeders of long coated varieties often choose to keep their stock in all-wire enclosures or at least enclosures with a false bottom of wire mesh which allows the animal's droppings to pass through and thus prevents the fur getting stained or dirty. Laboratory-bred animals are often housed in a similar manner to prevent infection if possible in the line-bred controlled stock. Cleanliness is extremely important to all pets, but such extreme precautions are not necessary to the average pet keeper. It is not the usual practice of Guinea Pig breeders to disturb a nest of mother and young until they are several days old, and therefore thorough cleaning should be postponed if necessary for a few days. A further help when cleaning is to cover the bare floor of the hutch with newspaper before laying on the sawdust. The paper can then often be removed complete with all the waste materials although if left for several days it can get wet and then is liable to stick to the bottom of the hutch, and will probably tear when being lifted. Alternative bedding materials can be used instead of hay. Straw may be used but unless this is clipped into short lengths it becomes very unwieldy. You should never use rags or other similar materials for bedding.

One of the nicest ways of housing Guinea Pigs is to keep them in colonies, that is groups of several adults in the one housing. To do this you need to provide good sized sleeping quarters leading off from an even larger exercise run. The exact size depends on your own ideas of stock levels but size can be based on the idea of using the same proportions as the hutch.

If you have a patch of grass available then construct your run and sleeping quarters in such a way as to make use of the grass as part of the exercise space. The addition of two handles at each end will enable you to move the enclosure on to other areas of grass when and if this is necessary. Wire across the bottom of such an enclosure may well prevent rats or some other creatures tunnelling through and stealing food or even killing the pets and the grass will grow through and hide the wire within a very short time.

Chapter 3

Feeding

It is possible to buy a balanced diet of foods in pellet form which, with the addition of drinking water, is sufficient to keep Guinea Pigs alive and healthy. Some commercial breeders and laboratory suppliers use this method, but although for effortless pet keeping this type of feeding goes a long way towards the ideal, nevertheless this is not the reason pet keepers take up the interest. Well balanced diets are necessary, but a diet of all of one type of food, no matter how nutritious, would be dull and uninteresting to most people and this applies equally to pets. Guinea Pigs can suffer from vitamin deficiency in the same way as other animals and vitamin C is as important to Guinea Pigs as it is to man. Without this vitamin scurvy can take hold of the animal in just the same way as ancient seamen suffered when on long voyages without fresh vegetables and fruit.

Greenstuff in the form of cabbage, cauliflower leaves, even grass and hay should form part of the diet and a handful of fresh hay given twice each day is a good supplement. Pellets can be fed in hoppers or food bowls if required, but they should never be fed in the wire feeders such as is used for some other rodents, as Guinea Pigs do not have mouths that can feed satisfactorily from this type of container.

Probably the most popular diets made up for Guinea Pigs is a mixture of rolled or crushed oats, bran, crushed maize and other cereals. This mixture can be made into a stodgy pudding-like mash with the addition of warm water which is enjoyed by some specimens particularly in cold weather, or, as most pet keepers feed the mixture, in bowls, dry and with no additives. Many pet dealers supply a mixture ready made up for Guinea Pigs or will make the mixture up for you. This means that you can ask for more of one ingredient than another in the mix, if you find your animals have particular preferences. Usually these mixtures contain some pelleted food also, but only accept pellets made up for rabbits and cavies and not poultry food, also try to make sure the pellets are fresh and green as they lose some of their vitamins if stored for long periods.

The food dishes should always be of the unspillable type where possible and made from pottery or similar materials that are easily cleaned. The teeth of rodents are very strong and even the metal tubes of drinking bottles can be pierced and crushed into a useless state. Plastics are not at all suitable for feeding or watering dishes. The cavy is known to blow into as well as suck out of the drinking bottle and this can cause blocking of the tube. Daily checking is recommended.

Although normally Guinea Pigs take much of the fluid they need from greenstuffs, they do need fresh water to drink and if fed on a pellet diet this is particularly important. Guinea Pigs are inclined to foul up the water by blowing bits of food etc. back up the drinking tubes and for this reason the water must be changed daily, regardless of how clean or how full the bottle appears to be. Because they are inclined to stand inside their food bowls, these too, need regular attention. All food must be fresh, especially green foods and any dirty or doubtful foods, leaves or fruit, must be thrown away.

Chapter 4

Handling and Sexing Guinea Pigs

Lifting very young Guinea Pigs presents no problems as they can be lifted with one hand then supported by the other hand. However, adult Guinea Pigs and particularly pregnant sows need extra care. Young people ought to be shown the proper way to pick up a pet and not be allowed to scoop up the animal allowing it to flop on each side of the hands, this usually causes pressure on the animal's abdomen.

The correct way to pick up your pet is to place one hand across the shoulders of the Guinea Pig, with the thumb behind the front leg on one side. The fingers then fall naturally into place over the shoulders and across the back of the animal and are well forward, curling just underneath the rib cage. Then gripping but not too firmly, the lifting begins and the other hand is put under the animal's rump to give support for the remainder of the lifting operation. Extra care is necessary when large or pregnant Guinea Pigs have to be lifted.

Commonsense should be used when handling all animals.
Grabbing them under the belly can injure them. Over the
shoulders with one hand and the other supporting the rump is
recommended for cavies.

Sexing Guinea Pigs is fairly easy at any age, though it is helpful
if someone with experience demonstrates the differences and the
procedure. After lifting the animal turn it onto its back with its
weight supported by the palm of the hand. With the fingers and
thumb of the other hand put gentle pressure on either side of
the genitalia. Moving the finger and thumb slightly apart will
extrude the papillae of the boar (male) pig quite easily, sows
(females) of course, have no such extrusion.

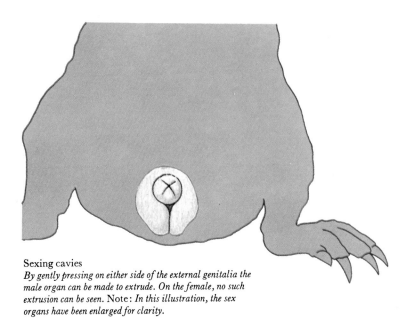

Sexing cavies
By gently pressing on either side of the external genitalia the male organ can be made to extrude. On the female, no such extrusion can be seen. Note: In this illustration, the sex organs have been enlarged for clarity.

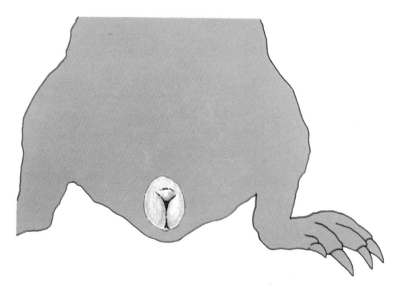

Chapter 5

Choosing and Buying your Guinea Pig

Unfortunately most beginners in the hobby will probably visit a local pet store and buy the first animal that appeals to them and very often this can lead to difficulties at a later date. Few people can resist the smallest of a litter or the Guinea Pig that appears to be shy or bullied by the others and though this does not necessarily mean that the animal is ill, nevertheless it is certainly the weakest animal and may have less chances of survival than the others in the same display cage. Therefore, do try to resist this temptation which may lead to a disappointment at a later stage, particularly if the pet is for a child.

Since you are now about to take on the responsibility for at least one other life, then choosing the animal is most important. Starting with healthy stock is very important as beginners may be unable to recognise symptoms of ill-health and then neglect can cause the loss of the pet. Pet dealers often buy their stock from casual suppliers, someone calls into the premises who has a few extra Guinea Pigs to dispose of and the pet dealer strikes a bargain. No matter what the price offered, few people want to take the animals home again and often accept a low price. The animals are then sometimes put in with existing stock (which may not be Guinea Pigs) and any problems that the stock may have can be transferred from one animal to the next. Also, even if the pet dealer tries to separate the sexes of his stock, very often he relies on the supplier and just puts them into the appropriate cages. The pet keeper may well buy a pregnant Guinea Pig without knowing it.

It must be stressed at this point that not all pet shop keepers behave in this way. Many of them are most particular about the stock that they put on sale and can be relied upon for their knowledge of the stock and how to look after it. This applies throughout the world.

It is recommended that if you are looking for your first pet Guinea Pig you should spend some time examining the sources of supply and the breeds and visiting several pet shops and forming an impression of the dealer's knowledge and integrity before buying a pet.

A much better and safer method of buying a Guinea Pig is to make contact with an enthusiast and then take their advice. Such a person may advertise in magazines devoted to the fur and feather pet trade, local papers or even on cards in shop windows. Others can be contacted at exhibitions or through specialist societies that cater for the enthusiast. This method of getting your first stock may be more difficult but it is certainly more beneficial to the new pet owner. Nothing counts as much as experience and all pet enthusiasts with experience are willing to share this with others, for the benefit of the hobby. They will not sell from poor stock, neither will they overcharge for their surplus animals.

However, since most established hobbyists will keep their animals for exhibition, it is extremely doubtful that you will be able to buy a potential prize winner very inexpensively. The animals you will be offered may fall slightly short of the ideal standard for that breed, perhaps the colour marking is wrong or the nose is not quite the right shape; these minor faults need not worry the pet keeper, and the animals should be perfectly healthy. A breeder will know the history of each animal in his collection and will probably be able to show you the parents as well as other relatives of your pet. Should you wish, the breeder will also probably show you the type of animal to breed with to eliminate the slight exhibition faults that the surplus animal may have. Buying a pair of unrelated animals from a breeder means that you could also be on the way to line-breeding and producing a champion.

Choice of breeds is a subject which depends on several factors. The availability of stock, the price (though there is seldom a great variation in price), plus the facilities you can provide for the pets, the time for caring for them that you have available and, probably the most important factor, which breed takes your fancy most. The wild Cavy has a speckled agouti coloured coat and it is from this basic coloured animal that all the variety of breeds at present available are descended.

The Silver Agouti – *is probably nearer the colouring of its wild ancestors than any other variety. Show specimens, however, must have its dark coloured body, 'ticked' with silver/white hairs in as even a pattern as possible and the belly line of the cavy is of the same lighter colour.*

It is not possible to describe or even list with accuracy all the breeds available today mainly because there is a constant effort by breeders all around the world to produce a new breed and such a list would be outdated very soon, even if it were practical to contact all the breeders. However, the hobby has recognised standards for exhibition Guinea Pigs and many recognisable breeds are available even to the casual buyer at a pet store. The agouti pattern of the original stock has remained popular with breeders, though the texture and background colour of the coat has been modified by line-breeding. The basic colours are silver and gold and both breeds have dark coats ticked with lighter coloured hairs, producing an even, overall pattern. The underside of the animals are an overall basic colour; like some other breeds they do not always breed true and produce some unexpected results in the colour of their offspring, referred to as 'sports'.

The Tortoiseshell-and-White Cavy – *is a smooth-coated variety and breeders aim for a chequered pattern of black, red and white each colour on one side of the body relating to a different colour on its opposite side. One of the most demanding of breeds for exhibitors and many youngsters, like the one illustrated, that do not reach the standards, end up as pets for children.*

A number of breeds are of just one basic colour all over and can be shades of black and white, cream, chocolate, red and even lilac colours; these breeds are known as 'selfs' and are smooth-coated. Marked or patterned smooth-coated Guinea Pig breeds include Dutch, where the rump is a different colour from the rest of the body, which is white, and patches of the contrasting colour appear on either side of the head of this breed. Tortoiseshell and white is a popular breed and a challenge to the breeder who will try to breed a champion with a chequered patterned coat contrasting one side with the other.

The Black Self Cavy – *is popular and like all other 'self' coloured animals, is the same colour all over its body. The coat is short and silky and has to be groomed to remove loose or miscoloured hairs that may occur. The shape of this animal is most important and it should have what is described by breeders as 'a bold Roman nose'.*

The rough coated varieties are just as popular and can be acquired in a variety of colours and patterns. The so-called Abyssinian breed is recommended for beginners and has been bred with 'Rosettes' formed by the unusual spread of the coat of the animal. Usually about four 'Rosettes' down each side of the Guinea Pig's tough, harsh coat.

The Abyssinian Cavy – has a harsh, rough coat forming a series of rosettes down the length of the body. The strong hairs form a ridge down the back of the cavy and this is crossed by a shoulder ridge and a rump ridge. The rough hair on the head and face give the cavy a bristly 'moustache'. It is a hardy animal requiring less grooming than other varieties.

The Peruvian variety has been bred with an extremely long coat which is parted down the centre of its back with some hair brushed over its face. The extended hair growth can often assume a length of 20 cms or more. From a beginner's point of view this breed is not always recommended. Such animals need fairly constant attention to coat and hutch conditions in order to keep the animal clean and healthy. Many prize specimens spend their entire lives with their long hair in paper tubes except when being judged or groomed and are made to live in hutches with false floors of wire mesh through which their droppings fall.

The Himalayan Cavy – *has a soft silky coat of pure white, with coloured areas on its nose, ears and feet. This colouring is not apparent at birth and does not fully develop until the animal is quite mature. Breeders of this variety have to be patient when waiting to see if they have a likely prize-winner, but may get rid of some stock early, simply because the shape of the head or some other anatomical feature is wrong.*

The Black Dutch – *is another difficult cavy to breed to reach show standards. Although even those not up to show standards are very attractive animals. They are smooth coated animals and the contrasting black and white colour markings are divided into two main areas. The head markings are even on each side, and the rump and back legs of the Dutch breeds are completely coloured except for the feet, which have small white 'socks'.*

The Orange Dutch – *is marked in the same way as the black variety. The head markings should meet just above the ears and the colour extend each side over the cheeks. The nose band of white extends up to the middle point between the ears in a triangle. The saddle area should be pure white, as are the front feet.*

Finally, before buying just one pet, consider taking a partner of either sex for the animal to live with. It is unlikely that the animal has previously lived in isolation and it is equally unlikely that the pet owner will always be able to spend time with the pet, in any case too much handling may upset the Guinea Pig until it gets used to it. Try to imagine how life would be for yourself if you were the only person around, and remember it is only slightly more trouble to keep two animals when you already have one.

The Peruvian Cavy – *is one variety not recommended for beginners; its long hair needs much grooming and frequent baths. Sometimes show specimens are kept with their coat wrapped in paper folded around the long hair and secured with elastic bands. On the day of the show, the animal's coat is then brushed out with a parting down its body and a fringe of hair over the animal's head.*

Chapter 6

Caring for your Pet

Guinea Pigs are fairly shy creatures when they are brought into a new environment and undoubtedly the best way to overcome this shyness is to allow them to get to know you gradually. Regular handling of the animal soon gives it the confidence it needs to remain calm when being given any attention. Unfortunately, most people when they acquire a pet for the first time continually pick it up and put it down and show it off to friends until they themselves are either tired or else find something different to give their attention to. The pets are usually tired long before this and may be hungry or thirsty without the new owner realising this.

When newly acquired, pets should be given routine attention which, with perhaps a few exceptions, can be kept to throughout its lifetime; its meals should be given at or around the same time each day, with some handling on each occasion. The main basic meal can be given in the evening and tit-bits, greenstuffs etc. in the morning. Depending on the pet keeper's own daily routine, an examination of the animal to evaluate its general condition can be done on either occasion. Experience will soon teach the owner what sort of condition the animal is in and whether it needs special attention or not. Soon it becomes almost second nature to the pet keeper to just look at his pet and tell at a glance that something is wrong. Pregnant sows should not be handled unnecessarily for obvious reasons.

Either during the morning or evening routines, the corner of the hutch used by the animals as a 'toilet' can be cleaned out and a handful of fresh sawdust to replace the soiled sawdust is all that is necessary. In large hutches or colony systems such daily cleaning may be less convenient or even unnecessary and it is a matter of personal judgement how the job is dealt with.

Some animals will eat their bedding, particularly if fresh meadow hay has been provided and therefore this must be replaced if necessary. Another point to watch for and which is easily overlooked by pet keepers and seldom remarked upon even by experts, is the fact that no matter how sheltered the sleeping quarters are, the position of the hutch in relation to the prevailing wind and weather conditions, is extremely important. Some animals will not sleep where they are supposed to, and many sleep in the open part of the hutch all night using the sleeping quarters only to deposit their droppings. It only takes a few days to sort out your pet's regular routine and you can make minor changes to your own methods and practices to suit those of the Guinea Pigs. This should not become a worrying factor, the animal will have enough natural sense to move back into the sleeping quarters if it gets too cold or even too hot. However, put the bedding where the animal sleeps.

Each day the food pot should be emptied, otherwise stale food may be left at the bottom, hidden by the topping up food put in. It has been said that Guinea Pigs often jump into their food pots and therefore droppings will be found amongst left over food. Washing and thoroughly drying the food bowl daily is a good routine to get used to, duplicating feed bowls is of course, a much easier routine in many ways. That is you replace each bowl daily with one collected the previous day and washed and dried when convenient.

Water bottles are more of a problem as they have to be taken off the wire front of the cage, emptied, washed out, filled and replaced each day. Dirt collects in the drinking tubes, around the bottle tops and sometimes in the bottles themselves. To remove this dirt successfully, the only practical answer is to use a bottle brush or test tube cleaner available at any stores which sell bottle feeders for babycare. Some water bottles supplied to the pet trade become easily clogged up and it is essential to check that your pet can drink whenever necessary. Also the most usual way of securing water bottles to wire fronts is by means of elastic and wire clips supplied by the manufacturers. This is not always very safe for two main reasons. Firstly, in the open air or dry conditions the elastic can perish and break and the result is often a broken bottle when it is rapidly released and sent to the ground. Also, some animals have been known to chew the elastic with the same results, or possibly worse if the clip is catapulted at the same time towards the Guinea Pig. Therefore, check these fastenings regularly; don't get careless and forget them.

As an alternative you could make a stronger, permanent fastening for feeding bottles by bending stiff wire around the bottle and then hooking this to the cage. Wire cut from coat hangers supplied from dry cleaners is particularly useful and can be bent and cut with simple tools.

Once a week the animals (except for very pregnant sows) should be removed and the whole hutch cleaned out. Using a hand brush with stiff bristles and a small shovel and a bucket the job is soon done. Making a useful scraper is something else that most people can do using only simple tools. You can use a triangular piece of sheet metal, cut from a tin lid or a box and punch a hole through the centre with a nail, then screw the scraper blade to a short piece of broom handle or similar piece of wood and there you have a scraper. Easier still is to buy a garden hoe and adapt this.

Once the hutch has been cleaned out, the new materials such as sawdust bedding etc. can be put in. The waste materials can be put to use in the garden. If they are kept in a heap and allowed to rot-down they can be used as a useful compost for plants, providing much needed bulky humus. During the weekly clean up the animals can be inspected more thoroughly than during the usual day-to-day inspections. Overgrown claws can then be dealt with, and teeth inspected in case they are overgrown, broken or damaged in any way. Ears and eyes should be examined for signs of ill health; husks from oats and other cereals can cause problems with Guinea Pigs should they get stuck in an ear. Guinea Pigs pick up parasites occasionally and these must be looked for and dealt with. This routine takes less than one minute each week for each animal and can save a great deal of trouble that might occur if problems go unnoticed or neglected.

Chapter 7

Breeding and Rearing

There is probably nothing more pleasing to the pet keeper than to see their pets caring for youngsters and watching these young animals mature. A great deal of learning about the animals and their behaviour takes place during this time.

However, although Guinea Pigs are easily encouraged to re-produce and the care of the young is usually without problems, all prospective pet breeders must decide at the very outset and before they commence a breeding programme why they want to breed from their pets. Few people make money from breeding pets on a home industry scale, the best you can hope for is to recoup some of the feeding expense by selling a few surplus young to friends, other enthusiasts or pet dealers, and so breed-ing for profit is not very practical unless you provide an inten-sive breeding programme and have a regular outlet for your stock.

Breeding for exhibition purposes is a different problem. Here line-breeding, cross-breeding and matching prospective parents, keeping accurate accounts and records are of utmost importance and even on this specialist side of the hobby problems arise when trying to dispose of unwanted stock not quite up to exhi-bition standards.

Most hobbyists, however, will want to breed from their stock at some time or other even if only to enlarge their own collection. If only a few specimens are bred then there is generally not too much bother to get rid of a few, although most Guinea Pigs reproduce in the spring and summer months and then everyone has surplus stock to unload on the pet dealer and this keeps prices down to a minimum.

The female Guinea Pig matures very early and can conceive at one month old. However, it is very unwise to allow such early breeding as the youngsters produced are often weaklings and the mother is inclined to neglect the first litter. The best age for a sow to be mated for the first time is said to be at about three months old and for the male just a few weeks younger.

In commercial breeding units a boar may serve as many as five or six sows in a colony; in a pet keeper's enclosure a trio of one boar and two sows is to be recommended. Some breeders recommend taking the sows away to separate nursing quarters once mating is known to have taken place, although many people keep the boar running with the females all the time. This means that as soon as the youngsters are born mating takes place again and whilst one litter is being suckled another is developing within the mother. Although some prolonged delay may well take place before the next youngsters are born, nevertheless this type of breeding will weaken the mother. Apart from this, Guinea Pigs are fairly 'highly-strung' animals and intensive breeding with more than one other sow and several families may well upset the community and cannibalism or sheer neglect may take place.

The gestation period is a long one, usually around 70 days, although it can vary a few days either way. The young litter (usually 2–4 of them) are born fully furred and with eyes and ears open – looking like miniature editions of their parents, although they may not have the same colour markings. They should not be disturbed for about three or four days and then they can be safely handled. They take milk from their mother until they are two and a half weeks old at which time they can be taken away from the mother and are said to be weaned. Guinea Pigs will often nibble solid foods at only one day old and will increase the amount of solids taken each day until weaned. At this stage they should be sexed and separated, otherwise mating is bound to take place. Extra benefit for the expectant and suckling sow can be gained by offering bread soaked with milk as a tit-bit. Dried hard crusts of bread and even twigs from fruit trees are also appreciated by Guinea Pigs as a treat and exercises their teeth.

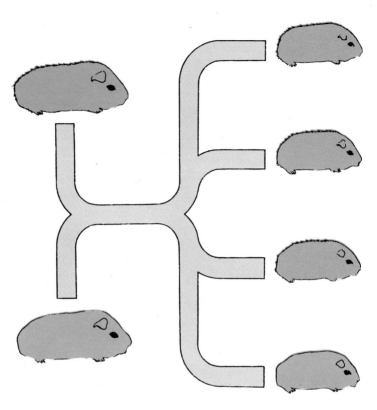

Pure bred rough coat adult mated with pure bred smooth coat

Pure bred dark coat mated with pure bred white

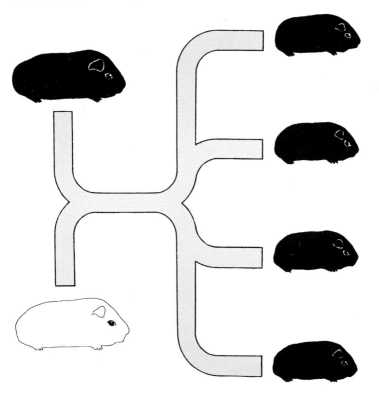

For any serious minded breeder, the importance of inheritance cannot be over-stressed, nor unfortunately, can the subject of heredity be easily understood at a casual glance.

As a science, heredity has been studied and written about for hundreds of years and still there is a great deal to learn. To study heredity, vast sums of money has been used: mating animals with short gestation periods and crossing the off-spring back and forth under controlled experimental conditions. New colours, shapes and sizes have developed until some of the varieties that are now common among pet keepers such as the Bengalese finch have no truly identified ancestors. In cavies, at least the wild ancestors are still known to exist, though they may look very different from the specimens seen on the show-bench. This demonstrates the point that by inter-breeding you can in theory change almost any animal into any shape, size or colour. However, this is not true in practice, by inter-breeding extensively in order to produce one element such as hair growth, you are very likely to be also changing another part of the animal's make-up which although not visible may be affecting the animal in an entirely different way and perhaps killing off the strain or giving the off-spring a serious malformation from which it may never recover.

Reproduction in cavies involves the union of sex cells, each parent giving one part of its make up to each cell. As the animal develops, each individual cell that becomes part of the animal as it grows carries chromosomes from both its father and its mother and therefore if you mate a pure-bred black cavy to a pure-bred white cavy, all the young carry a chromosome which itself carries a coat factor for black from one parent and for white from the other. *But* when they are born, the young all appear black. The factor or genes for black coats are in fact dominant and mask those genes which are for white. However, if two of the 'black' youngsters are mated, black and white young appear at a ratio of three that appear black to one white. Out of four young cavies born in this way, however, only one is pure black, two appear black but have mixed genes both black and white and one has no black genes at all and therefore is born white.

Quite separately there are genes which are again paired and split when the cavies mate that are concerned with other anatomical details such as texture, and length of coat. In fact, a rough coated cavy mated with a smooth-coated cavy if both are pure-bred, would produce all rough-coated young because rough-coated genes are dominant to smooth-coated ones.

If you take this a stage further and mate a rough-coated white with a smooth-coated black, then you can just begin to see how so many different varieties of cavies have been developed. Going beyond this becomes more complicated each time you introduce a new factor and as has been pointed out, close inbreeding, i.e. mating brother and sister, brings out inherent weaknesses and is not at all recommended. Occasionally an experienced breeder will do this in order to extract a particular factor or strengthen one. The immediate task then is to breed back strength into the off-spring and even if the breeder is successful it may take several generations. Therefore, before any breeding programme is carried out it is wise to find out from the dealer or previous owner of the cavies about their ancestry. Providing the animals are not closely related, mating them will do no harm if they are mature, but you may be surprised by the results.

It is highly recommended that any beginner talks to someone with experience before breeding. No enthusiast wants to see a breed spoiled simply because of careless breeding. If you want to breed long-haired cavies, try to get parents that have already been bred to achieve long hair, do not try to start at the beginning again and waste all the efforts that have been put in before you. However, your own efforts can improve the breed in some way and for the ambitious, a programme for breeding a particular inherent factor to improve the stock may take many years, but nevertheless you are then on the way to having your own noteworthy strains and that is an achievement.

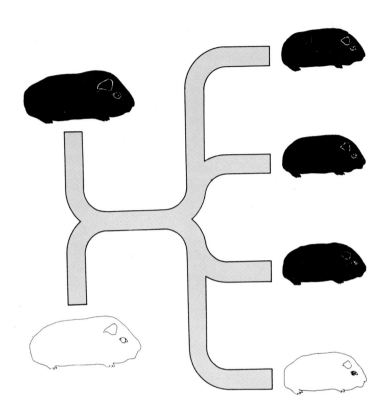

Cross bred young mated

Chapter 8

Exhibiting

The advantages of supporting exhibitions are more obvious to the experienced breeder than to the beginner. The experienced person will want to demonstrate how good he or she is at line-breeding and selective matching of the stock to achieve a required standard. This approach to the hobby benefits the pet keeper as well as the expert since the wider choice of really good Guinea Pigs recently available is entirely due to the efforts of dedicated people. The prizes to be won even at national level are usually quite modest, perhaps only a showcard or at best a small cup and a small amount of prize money.

The real pleasure is gained from mixing with fellow enthusiasts and discussing the various points of the animals on show and even disagreeing (in the friendliest way) with the judges' decisions. A well turned out animal can be a real joy to the owner, particularly if admired by other enthusiasts and the time and trouble taken to produce a good exhibit is then well rewarded.

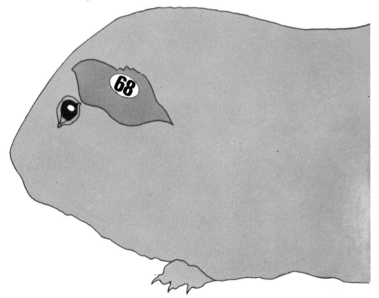

When entering a cavy for a show, you will be issued a small self-sticking label bearing the exhibit number that corresponds to the number on the pen in which the cavy will be kept until the judging takes place, after which it is returned to the pen. The label is usually placed behind the cavy's ear and is not at all harmful.

Cavies usually arrive early in the morning of a big show and are penned by the owner who gives no indication to the judges or stewards as to which animal is owned by him or her. The recording steward appoints the pen numbers and these are kept secret until after the final judging. The owner is allowed to put food, hay, water, etc., into the pen, but usually only does this after judging, otherwise the animal may get wet and dirty.

Preparing for a show is fairly straightforward. Firstly the animals should be got used to being handled. A frightened, jumpy specimen is not likely to be given as thorough examination by the judge as one which is easily handled and tame. The smooth coated varieties can be bathed a few days before the exhibition and a day later, when the coat is still soft, the loose guard hairs (the longer coat hairs) are brushed out with a damp sponge or just a hand that has been made wet with clean water. This causes the loose hairs to stick and lift out. Some experts tweak the guard hairs out by hand but this is a bit tricky for a beginner. Both the Abyssinian and the Peruvian breeds are bathed a few days before the show and the coat brushed into shape with a fairly soft-bristled brush as is used for small babies.

To bathe a Guinea Pig, use warm (not hot) water in a sink or basin of suitable size and lower the animal into this, supporting its body until its feet rest on the bottom, the water should not need to be more than 5 or 6 cm deep. Using a mildly medicated shampoo wet the animal's fur and gently massage the coat with the shampoo and water, keeping the mixture away from the animal's head, particularly the eyes and ears. Rinse thoroughly and repeat the process once more. After the second rinse dry the animal with a towel and brush the coat into shape. Some animals feel insecure on a smooth surface such as a sink or basin and a piece of cloth or a towel laid in the bottom of the sink, (under the water) sometimes helps the animal to settle and feel secure.

Shows are governed by national as well as local rules and these may vary in each country and to a certain extent from show to show. Anyone wishing to exhibit must abide by the rules appertaining to that show and a newcomer should seek advice when entering a Guinea Pig for the first time and filling in the entry form. Different classes are held for young and adult animals, Boars and Sows, varieties and breeds and so on. Class winners are entered in best of breed, best Sow, best Boar and best in show, to become show champion.

The exhibits are usually assigned to individual cages and

labelled with a small stick-on label placed behind the ear of the animal. No other form of labelling is permitted. Show stewards carry the animals to the judges who judge the animals according to the recognised show standards for that particular breed.

After the judging and the prizes have been awarded, competitors are then free to discuss the merits of their Guinea Pigs and can learn a great deal at this time. Exhibitions often take place within local agricultural shows or similar events and sometimes after the judging animals are put up for sale. This is one of the best methods of acquiring knowledge of the breeds and buying your first stock and is highly recommended. At these shows local clubs exhibit and enrol new members on the spot. Never be afraid to ask advice about the hobby from the exhibitors as they are usually very willing to help. However, they are enthusiasts and may take up a great deal of time explaining all the subtle points about the joy of keeping Guinea Pigs or Cavies as they prefer to call them when at exhibitions.

Chapter 9

Illness or Health Problems

Almost every chapter covering this subject in all pet books begins with the statement that 'prevention is better than cure' and this is very true in all cases. Fortunately, Guinea Pigs are not particularly susceptible to illness and if kept on a healthy mixed diet and housed in comfortably dry conditions, it is unlikely that any sickness or other health problems will occur.

However, some animals may catch cold due to accidental chilling or exposure to other sick animals and such chills should be treated with common sense as much as anything. The first signs are probably the lethargic appearance of the pet, wet discharge from the nose and perhaps damp around the eyes. Such an animal should be isolated, kept warm but not hot and given warm milk with bread (preferably brown bread) soaked in it, in addition to the normal diet and plenty of water. If there is no improvement after three days consult an experienced pet keeper or veterinarian.

Sometimes Guinea Pigs are afflicted by fleas or lice; this is fairly rare but these parasites can be brought in with hay from time to time. Treatment with an insecticide powder is simply a matter of dusting the animal without getting the powder in its eyes and in fact if you just dust the back, belly and rump of the animal, this should be enough. After 4–5 days a second dusting should prove enough for the most persistent fleas.

Overgrown claws can be clipped at home but very strong clippers are essential and since the method requires some skill and knowledge of anatomy, it is wisest to have this operation demonstrated before any attempt is made by yourself. This last statement applies even more in the case of overgrown teeth.

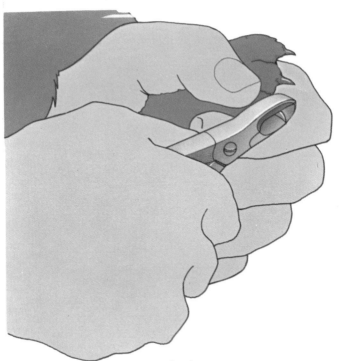

The claws of cavies do overgrow occasionally and can be clipped by the owner. However, there is a vein running down inside each claw and this cannot be seen in the dark claws of some animals. Before attempting to do-it-yourself, seek expert advice.

Sometimes animals develop sores or patches of bald, damaged skin for no apparent reason. This could be due to a diet deficiency or an allergy of some kind and needs the expert treatment of a veterinarian and should not be ignored since it may just be contagious.

In laboratory bred animals many more illnesses and diseases appear in the stock from time to time but in the pet trade these are rare but occasional lumps which turn out to be harmless tumours occur in pets and these can be removed by a veterinary surgeon, though it is seldom inexpensive.

However, the responsibility to provide a good life for pets is entirely the owner's and this should be clearly understood at the outset.

Seed husks, dirt, etc., can get into the ears of these animals and cause irritation and may even become infected. A weekly check with a cotton stick or swab sold for use with babies is all that is usually necessary.

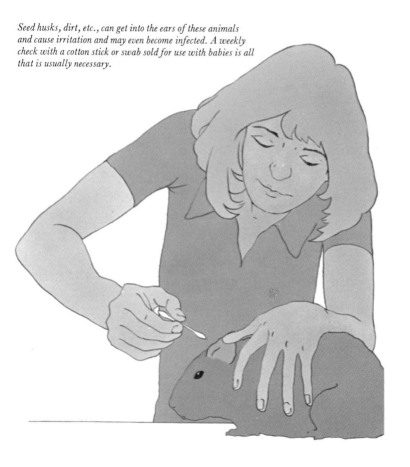

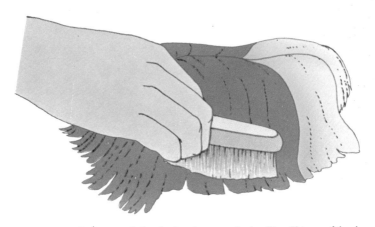

Cavies will enjoy being groomed after they have become used to handling. Using a soft brush designed for babies and young children's hair will add sparkle and polish to the coat and keep it free from dust, tangles and so on.

Part Two

Chinchillas

Chapter 1

History and Origins

The hobby side of keeping Chinchillas has increased in recent years and many people who have in the past kept Guinea Pigs or Rabbits have extended their interests to these animals. The reasons for this are probably due to the few adaptations that are necessary to change a routine for keeping Guinea Pigs to keeping Chinchillas.

Chinchillas are rodents and also like the ancestors of the domestic Guinea Pig are native to South America. The family known scientifically as CHINCHILIDAE contains only six species, all of which are native to South America, and includes the Visacha, the much larger, pampas-living animals whose hoards at their burrows include rubbish left behind by travellers as well as much vegetation, bones etc.

The Chinchilla is said to have the most valuable fur in the animal kingdom and it is for this reason that the many Chinchilla farms were started and flourished until recent years. Some farms still exist and the fine, soft fur pelts are matched and graded and sent to the furriers. Sometimes more than a hundred pelts are needed to make one coat. Previously the pelts were all taken from wild stock and the populations of these animals were almost wiped out, prior to the extensive breeding campaigns, such was the demand for the fur. Fortunately for the Chinchilla, fur coats are somewhat less fashionable at the present time and although the price of a Chinchilla is still often four or five times that of a Guinea Pig, nevertheless this is still as much as only one-tenth or even one-twentieth as expensive as they were at the height of their popularity about 20 years ago when even the dealers were paying hundreds of dollars for stock. The domèstication of the species has a very interesting history and the fur farms that developed in the U.S.A. and Canada all appear to have originated from stock supplied from an American mining engineer who set up a colony of eight males and three females in California in 1923.

The animal is extremely attractive appearing a little larger in body size than a Guinea Pig although, in fact, generally weighing less. The head is similar in shape to a Rabbit and though the ears are quite large they are rounded. The Chinchilla has a tail much like the Squirrel, but not quite so long and bushy. The hind legs are longer than the front legs and the animal progresses in a series of hops in a rabbit-like fashion; however, it can leap both horizontally and vertically and is extremely agile. The Chinchilla has unique fur, unlike any other animal, and is so dense that even when parted it is difficult to see the animal's skin. Each individual hair root gives rise to many hairs, sometimes as many as eighty from one root.

Chinchillas can become very tame and may even be allowed into the house for exercise during the evening when they are generally most active. Other domestic pets such as dogs and cats do not seem to worry them and both animals would find it difficult to catch a Chinchilla at speed. Nevertheless, individual animals differ and only when a pet keeper is confident about the reaction he is likely to get should any attempt be made to introduce strange animals to each other.

Chapter 2

Housing

In principle the same kind of housing requirements are required for both Chinchillas and Guinea Pigs, they must be damp-proof, draught-proof and protected from extremes of temperature. Most pet keepers prefer to keep their pets inside the house in a spare room or in a tool shed in the garden where the temperature can be kept above freezing point in the winter and can be kept cool in really hot weather. Chinchillas are not delicate animals, but in their natural state they could choose to move to a cooler or warmer place as best suited them and they dislike the hot sunshine of mid-day yet may like to sunbathe in the evening or early morning. In captivity they do not have this choice and therefore siting the hutches or cages is always an important factor.

Professional Chinchilla breeders keep their stock in all wire and metal cages with hopper feeders and water bottles hung on the sides. In some cases the male Chinchilla serves several females having a free run between several interconnected wire cages, whilst the females are restricted by plastic collars fitted around their necks to prevent them leaving their own enclosure. It should be emphasised that this is not a cruel practice and no harm or discomfort is placed upon the restricted animals. However, the professional can keep his stock well controlled, an important factor when considering the hundreds of animals that may be housed in one building or ranch.

For the person who would wish to keep only a few pets, wire cages such as the professionals use, although they keep the animals in good condition, do not allow as much freedom for observation of the pets and a much larger enclosure of wood and wire makes a great deal of difference to the activity of the Chinchillas. Nearly all wooden surfaces of the enclosure will be chewed by the Chinchillas, to a state of destruction in some cases. Therefore, exposed wood surfaces should be protected by wire netting if the animals are likely to be able to get their teeth into them. Protecting the floor surface is often unnecessary nor indeed any flat surface where the animal cannot get a start to its chewing process. A false bottom to the cage of wire, about 1 cm gauge, secured to a frame allows the droppings to pass through and reduces the possibility of the animal soiling its coat. A fairly solid sleeping box can be placed inside or hung on the outside of the cage for convenience, though this may well need replacement after constant chewing by the inmates. Some people claim that a smooth wooden floor does not offer enough grip for the animal when moving around, but if the surface is covered with sawdust or wood shavings then this problem is unlikely to be experienced.

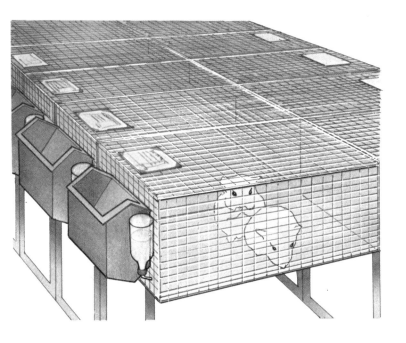

Commercial breeding cages

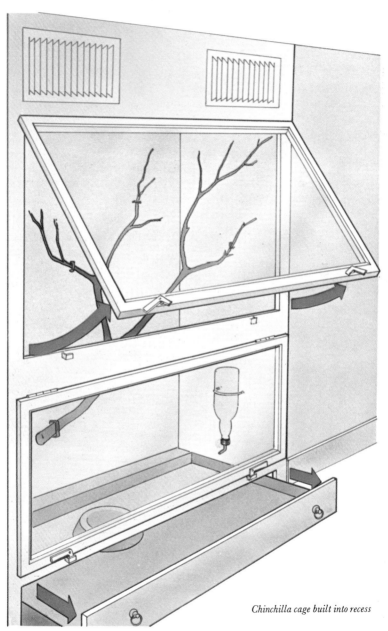

Chinchilla cage built into recess

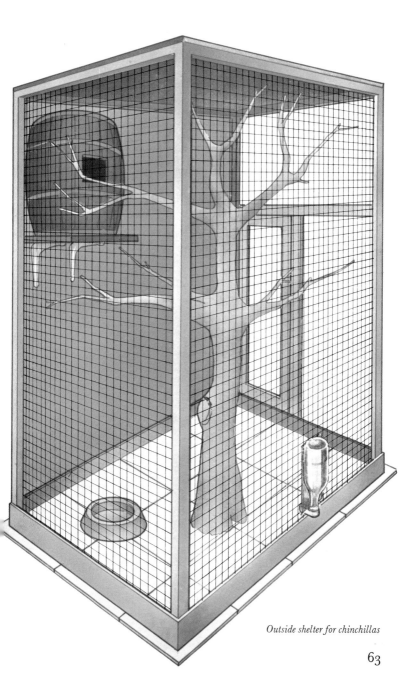

Outside shelter for chinchillas

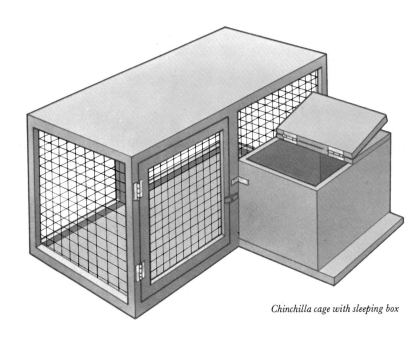

Chinchilla cage with sleeping box

Chinchillas are extremely agile and in order to allow them to demonstrate their agility, a tall cage with tree branches arranged at different heights makes an excellent showpiece and provides exercise whenever the animals feel the need.

All food bowls should be unspillable and although they seem to drink very little water if given enough greenstuff, the water bottle should always be available and kept full of clean water. One unusual item that will also need to go into the cage from time to time is a dust bath. Usually a large pie dish or baking tin serves this purpose, but it is important to remember this when building the cage, as all these items must be able to pass through the door easily and therefore a large door is important.

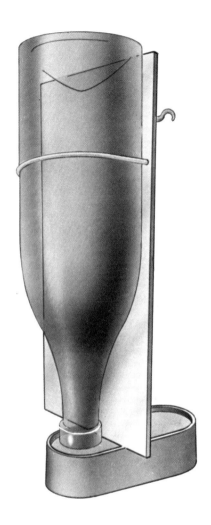

Not all chinchillas drink a great deal, but those on a dry pellet diet need to drink much more than those on a mixed diet. Water should always be available and with this type of water feeder the bottle remains outside of the cage with less risk of accidents and generally holds more than the smaller ones designed for pet use. Using a green wine bottle cuts down the light on the water and helps prevent growth of algae.

Chapter 3

Feeding

Professional breeders have now reached a stage where their animals are fed almost exclusively on a balanced diet of specially prepared pellets and a handful of hay each day for roughage (an important part of the Chinchilla's diet). Like other rodents, the Chinchilla's teeth are constantly growing and need a good hard surface to work upon to keep them trimmed to a useful length. Therefore, crisp, dried foods are essential and pellet foods should, if necessary, be dried off in an oven if they are not as hard as they should be.

Heavy food dish with overlapping top suitable for chinchilla. Also pumice stone to gnaw on

Other dried foods such as wheat, maize, barley, rolled oats, bran etc. can be used and are probably easier to obtain than pellets although less economical as a Chinchilla needs only about one heaped tablespoonful of pellets each day and much of the other foods may well be wasted. A spoonful of sunflower seeds once each week is a nice treat; peanuts, either shelled or otherwise, are another variation and depending on the availability other nuts can be offered. Fruit such as apples and pears add to the variety, plus raisins and other dried soft fruits.

Most rodents enjoy chewing at the twiggy branches of fruit trees and willow. Always ensure that no spraying for pests has been done to any such foods offered.

Of real benefit to the Chinchilla's teeth is the provision of the occasional tree branch or twigs and leaves from fruit or willow trees. Some people provide blocks of pumice or mineral salts to help wear the teeth down and this often prevents the animals from attacking the woodwork of their cages.

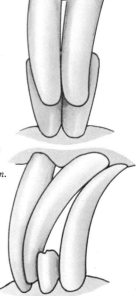

The teeth of the animals are extremely important and should be inspected once a week in case they are growing badly or otherwise mis-shapen. The teeth shown here are, in fact, drawn from a living animal that fell and broke a tooth. This remained unnoticed and as the teeth no longer meet properly, overgrowth has occurred, causing constant veterinary attention.

Chapter 4

Handling and Sexing Chinchillas

Because they are so quick and agile, Chinchillas are not as easy to catch as Guinea Pigs and in a large cage it is almost a case of trying to anticipate the next movement of the animal and then being quite ready to make a grab at the less tame specimens. Those which have been handled a great deal are less likely to panic when the cage is approached.

Chinchillas are not heavy animals, adults weighing about 2 lb when fully mature. The method of picking them up is to place the hand across the animal's shoulders with the thumb behind one front limb and the fingers curling over its back and under-

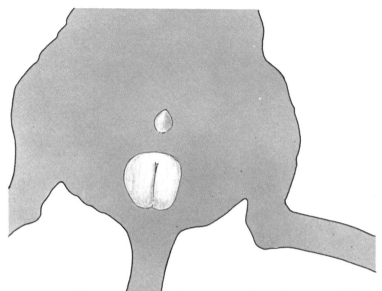

Sexing chinchillas takes a little practice as the organs are not always as clear to see as in this enlarged diagrammatic view. The male above has a wide gap between its sex organs, though not always as wide as illustrated here.

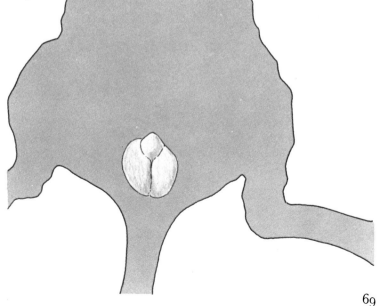

69

neath its body; gently with no pressure but with firmness the animal can be lifted and supported by the other hand. Eventually the animal will learn to sit on the hands without restraint.

Sexing Chinchillas needs practice and should be demonstrated by someone who has experience. The sex organs differ from Guinea Pigs' and although in adults the male sex organs are wider apart than in the female, this is not easily distinguished in young animals. Female Chinchillas have three vents and these are placed much closer together, but the middle vent is not always easy to see and careful examination is necessary.

Chapter 5

Choosing and Buying your Chinchilla

People who keep Chinchillas as pets seem to turn up in the most unlikely places. Professional breeders, however, can best be located through a national registry if one exists in your country, and some zoos and pet dealers will be able to offer advice. However, magazines and newspapers do carry advertisements offering them for sale and most of these people will send the animals by train or road to the purchaser, although for a beginner this is not a good idea, it is much better to see the animals before you buy them and get some really useful advice from the breeder before you take them into your care. A professional breeder, when buying new stock, will probably know the complete history of the animals offered, the strain and the line-breeding that has taken place, plus the standard or grade of pelt he can expect. Few breeders would sell stock that is unwell or deformed to a beginner though they may want to unload animals that are now too old to breed, although still have a life expectancy of 4–5 years. Such animals are usually less expensive than youngsters.

Pet dealers who display animals in their shops are less likely to know the animals' history or the state of the animals' health. Chinchillas should be bright and alert without messy coats, wide shining eyes and feeding well. However, during the daytime they are less energetic and therefore when bought from a pet store it is difficult to judge if they are just sleepy, chilled or unwell. If possible try to see them over several days if you are buying from an unreliable source or else better still, get a veterinary certificate of good health from the dealer. Chinchillas bought in this way are not inexpensive and therefore precaution must be taken to protect your investment.

Chinchilla breeders have a long way to go before they reach the many colour varieties now available in Guinea Pigs. Nevertheless, there are plenty to choose from, the basic slate blue/grey is an extremely attractive animal and the most well known, the beige is now well-established. Silver and cream Chinchillas are also available plus a white variety, though all these are more costly than the normal coloured Chinchilla.

Himalayan Chinchilla

Fawn Chinchilla

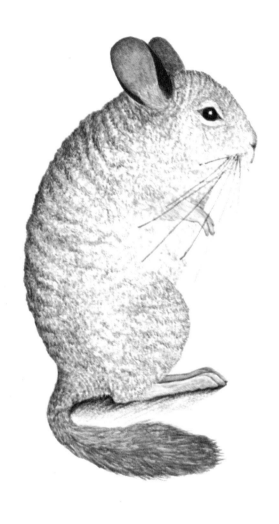

Silver Chinchilla

Chapter 6

Caring for your Chinchilla

The every-day needs of the Chinchilla are much the same as Guinea Pigs, they need comfortable housing, a good diet and cleanliness. If the cage has a false bottom of wire the droppings will fall through this and make cleaning the cage much easier. A metal drawer under the wire will make cleaning a great deal easier and can be made when the cage is designed and built.

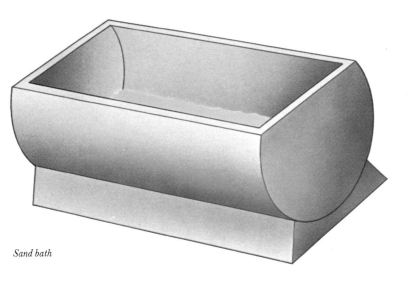

Sand bath

One feature of Chinchilla life which always provides entertainment for experienced keepers as well as newcomers is their love of a dust bath. This can be offered daily, but once or twice a week is usually enough. The bath itself is usually about 12″ long, 8″ wide and has a depth of 4″ (approximately 30 cm × 15 cm × 10 cm) and the dust, which consists of Fuller's earth or very, very fine powdered clay or sand, is placed in the bath to a depth of about 1″ (2·5 cm). The Chinchillas will ignore ordinary sand even if this is very fine, it must have a dust-like consistency and be very dry. When placed in the cage the Chinchillas jump in and roll over and over kicking up the dust as it rushes through their fur and thoroughly enjoying the sensation it gives them. This process removes debris from the fur, dries the fur and seems to polish it, leaving it fine, soft and with a sparkle. The bathing should take place before meals which are usually given in the evening. The bath is removed after about 30 minutes otherwise the dust may get contaminated unnecessarily with droppings, waste food etc., though this can be sieved out if necessary.

Chapter 7

Breeding

The general rules governing the breeding of Chinchillas apply to all other forms of animal husbandry. The animals must be in good condition at the right time, this means that working towards a breeding programme by correct feeding and housing the animals in clean, healthy conditions will be rewarded with strong, healthy youngsters.

The gestation period for Chinchillas is quite a long one being one hundred and eleven days, which means that for the pet keeper careful planning must be a consideration when attempting to breed. It would be unfortunate if the young were born when the owner was away on holiday or some similar occurrence caused the pet keeper to miss the event.

Unless you are going to breed on a colony system with one mate serving several females, then the Chinchillas can be paired up when they are about six months old and will usually live together for a lifetime. Pairing them off sometimes causes violent outbreaks but this is not common and if the Chinchillas in such a pairing continue to fight after a few trial minutes then it is wise to separate them and seek other mates. The colony system is much more difficult to control from the breeder's point of view when matching up the animals and fighting occurs.

It is not usual for the animals to mate in the daytime and so the pet keeper rarely sees this happening, nor is it likely that the female will show any signs of being on heat, which occurs for only a short time each month. The only reliable method of knowing when a mating has taken place is to look for the small, white sac or stopper that is passed by the female after mating. The precise function of this unusual mucous-filled sac is still a mystery to pet keepers. However, they are only noticed by really watchful hobbyists and experienced breeders and in a matter of hours shrivel up into hard, yellow deflated sacs. One other sign of a possible mating is that pieces of loose fur are found in the cage and it can be seen that these were pulled from the flanks or backs of the females. Any such signs should be recorded and then the possible date of birth can be calculated as approximately one hundred and eleven days away. At about half way through this period the female should have gained a few ounces in weight and this should be noticeable. Experienced stock breeders weigh their animals regularly and record the details on the animal's record card.

About two weeks before the birth is due the female can be given milk as an addition to her regular diet, which should be gradually increased as soon as the animal is known to be pregnant. Some breeders prefer to use a teaspoonful of powdered milk in the feed instead of wet milk that can get messy and soiled more easily. The female makes no nest, and about 8–10 days before the young are due, clean, short-cropped straw or hay should be provided in the nest box and kept topped up daily if eaten or scattered. At this time also, the daily dust bath is denied the female and not returned until some time after the birth when her sex organs appear normal. Even then the owner must ensure that the dust is not likely to cling to the animal's fur when she is suckling the young as this might get into their throats, nostrils and eyes.

The usual litter size is two but can be up to five although this number is rare. The very wet young, although fully formed with their eyes open, have to be kept dry and warm and the dry bedding helps very much; damp bedding must be changed. The youngsters will begin to nibble at solid food at about ten days old and grow quickly. They are finally weaned when about sixty days old and can be sexed and housed separately if necessary.

Females will often become pregnant very shortly after the litter is born if the male is still present and though this is not dangerous it does tend to put something of a strain on the female. Therefore, overbreeding of this kind is not advised and it is much wiser to allow the female to raise the young and then re-mate her. Although experts who breed for fur quality are inclined to interbreed to a certain extent by cross-matching related animals, this requires a degree of skill and knowledge of genetics beyond the scope of most beginners, therefore unrelated animals are recommended for breeding without complications or deficiencies occurring. Females are usually retired from breeding at about 4 years old and then continue for several more years as pets.

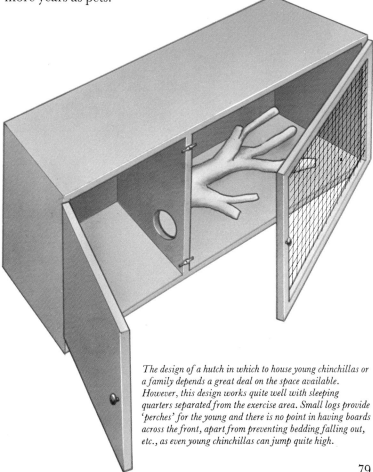

The design of a hutch in which to house young chinchillas or a family depends a great deal on the space available. However, this design works quite well with sleeping quarters separated from the exercise area. Small logs provide 'perches' for the young and there is no point in having boards across the front, apart from preventing bedding falling out, etc., as even young chinchillas can jump quite high.

Chapter 8

Exhibiting

Until comparatively recently there has been little interest in exhibiting Chinchillas in the same organised way as Guinea Pigs, Rabbits, Mice etc. In fact, even today the hobby is only just becoming established and for the present time exhibitions take place alongside classes for Guinea Pigs or Rabbits. Nevertheless, the interest appears to be on the increase and more hobbyists are taking their animals along to these otherwise restricted shows. In the past it was the dried pelt of the Chinchilla that was exhibited at fur trade shows or the live animals could be exhibited at pet shows either in children's pet classes or as unusual pets.

It takes quite a long time to develop the exhibition interest in any form of livestock and to evaluate the way in which the animals can be judged and to set ideal standards for the breeder to aim at. However, it seems likely that the continuation of the interest in Chinchillas as pets will soon provide enough exhibitors to warrant further development and that serious minded hobbyists will form committees and councils to formulate the rules of the 'fancy'. With this in mind the hobbyist with a desire to get into a developing area of pet keeping would probably do well to take up Chinchilla breeding, the opportunities must be there for anyone to become an established exhibitor and to develop a particular exhibition strain.

It should be realised, however, that the rewards for such endeavours are not of great financial benefit. Usually breeders of fancy pets for exhibition are considered fortunate if they make some money towards the costs of feeding their pets and seldom, if ever, make a real profit from pet keeping. The real reward for these people is that they have been able to prove their abilities in animal husbandry. They have selected the breeding stock on intuition backed by personal knowledge and through the right kind of attention have been successful in producing an animal considered better than the next exhibitor's. It is a real personal pride that keeps these hobbies going and although the competition is quite strong when the animals are being judged and feelings can run at a very high level between exhibitors who consider the judges' decision is not the right one. After the event such feelings are forgotten and the hobby continues to thrive, through the comradeship of its followers.

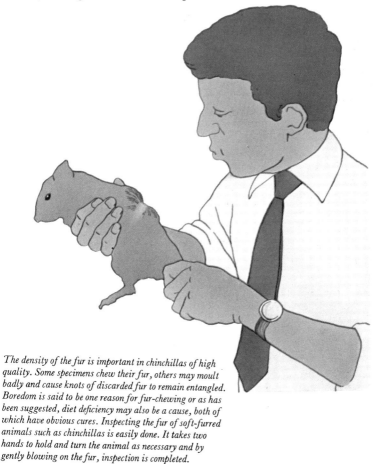

The density of the fur is important in chinchillas of high quality. Some specimens chew their fur, others may moult badly and cause knots of discarded fur to remain entangled. Boredom is said to be one reason for fur-chewing or as has been suggested, diet deficiency may also be a cause, both of which have obvious cures. Inspecting the fur of soft-furred animals such as chinchillas is easily done. It takes two hands to hold and turn the animal as necessary and by gently blowing on the fur, inspection is completed.

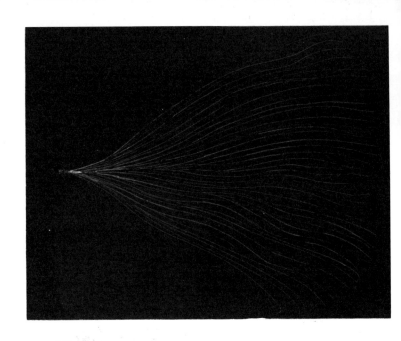

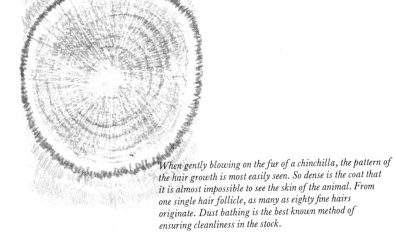

When gently blowing on the fur of a chinchilla, the pattern of the hair growth is most easily seen. So dense is the coat that it is almost impossible to see the skin of the animal. From one single hair follicle, as many as eighty fine hairs originate. Dust bathing is the best known method of ensuring cleanliness in the stock.

A family of Chinchillas

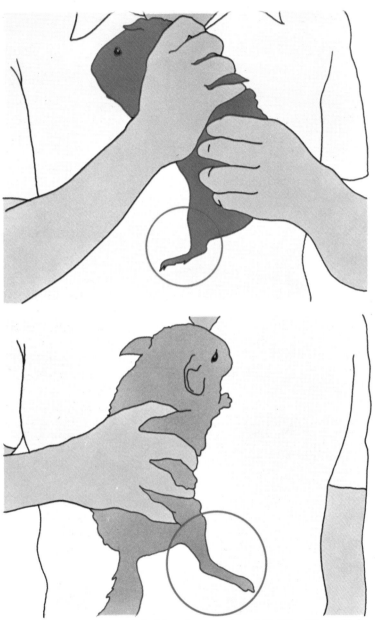

The length of the hind leg is markedly different between cavies and chinchillas. The long hind leg of the chinchilla enables it to jump and leap in kangaroo style at a remarkable speed.

Chapter 9

Health Problems

Animals that are kept in healthy conditions and on a well balanced diet rarely become ill, though sometimes new stock or a door or window left open can cause a chill or other illness among normally healthy stock. The Chinchilla fur is so thick and fine that parasites such as fleas cannot penetrate to the skin and feed and therefore this problem is not likely to be met with. Some animals chew their fur and this is unsightly, and though no conclusive evidence can be given for the cause, keeping the animals in dark, airless conditions is believed to be a contributing factor.

Constipation and diarrhoea are usually caused by incorrect feeding and housing and both are obvious signs to the experienced keeper that something is wrong with the usual routine. Constipated animals should be encouraged to drink and eat green food and fruit. Animals whose droppings are wet or loose should be kept on a drier diet and offered burnt toasted bread. Animals that catch colds are best treated in warm conditions with additional vitamins and warm milk offered in the diet. Scratches and cuts sometimes occur in animals and the reasons are varied but should be sought and recurrence prevented if possible. All wounds should be washed with warm water with just a little antiseptic fluid added; dust bathing should not be allowed whilst the animal has an open wound.

Fortunately, most mild illnesses and slight accidents can be treated by the pet keeper using common sense knowledge. However, the pet should not be allowed to suffer unduly and should be given the benefit of skilled veterinary advice if there is any reason to believe that the animal is seriously ill.

INDEX

INDEX